JOSÉ MARTÍ

MAN OF POETRY, SOLDIER OF FREEDOM

BY ALAN WEST

Hispanic Heritage
The Millbrook Press
Brookfield, Connecticut

Verses one, two, and four of the poem on page 22 were translated by Alan West; verse three was translated by Coley Taylor.

Library of Congress Cataloging-in-Publication Data
West, Alan, 1953–
José Martí, man of poetry, soldier of freedom / by Alan West.
p.m.—(Hispanic heritage)
Includes bibliographical references and index.
Summary: Tells the life story of the Cuban patriot and
poet. He organized the uprising that led to Spain's
withdrawal from Cuba, all the while blazing new trails
in Latin American literature.
ISBN 1-56294-408-8 (lib. bdg.)
1. Martí, José, 1853–1895—Juvenile literature. 2. Cuba—
History—1878–1895—Juvenile literature. 3. Revolutionaries—
Cuba—Biography—Juvenile literature. 4. Statesmen—
Cuba—Biography—Juvenile literature. 5. Authors, Cuban
—19th century—Biography—Juvenile literature. [1. Martí,
José, 1853–1895. 2. Cuba—History—1878–1895. 3.
Revolutionaries. 4. Authors, Cuban.] I. Title. II. Title:
Man of poetry, soldier of freedom. III. Series.
F1783.M38W47 1994 972.91'05'092—dc20 [B] 93-6258 CIP AC

Cover photo courtesy of The Granger Collection
Photos courtesy of The Bettmann Archive: pp. 3, 27; Center
for Cuban Studies: pp. 4, 7 (both), 11 (both), 13, 16,
21, 23, 24; Organization of American States: pp. 8, 20; The
Schomburg Center for Research in Black Culture, New York
Public Library: p. 9; New York Public Library: p. 29.

Published by The Millbrook Press
2 Old New Milford Road, Brookfield, Connecticut 06804

JOSÉ MARTÍ

Martí in prison. He sent a copy of this photo to his mother.

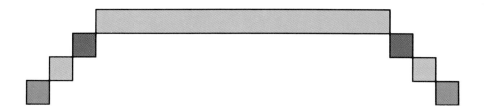

When *he was only seventeen*, José Martí, or Pepe, as he was known to his friends and family, went to prison. He was forced to work breaking rocks in a pit in the ground. The bright sun of tropical Cuba made the rocks blindingly white. Dust clouded the air and choked the young prisoner.

Pepe and the other inmates had to carry the heavy rocks. It was exhausting work. Any sign of weakness was met by the guard's whip. As Pepe worked, he felt the shackles around his ankle and waist dig into his flesh. Every moment reminded him of his own and his country's lack of liberty.

In Pepe's time, the late 1800s, Cuba belonged to Spain. The Spanish government made all the important decisions about Cuba's economy, its laws, and the way it was run. The Spanish also upheld slavery. Under Spanish rule many Cubans, most of them black and *taino* (Native Americans who lived on the island when the

Spanish arrived), were robbed of their freedom. They were forced to work on the farms of wealthy landowners who made the Spanish rich.

José Martí went to prison because he opposed Spanish rule, slavery, and injustice. The Spaniards hurt and confined his body, but not his spirit. Martí fought against them and their ways in both deed and word. He became a hero in the fight for Cuba's freedom. And he gave to the people of the Americas some of the most beautiful and lasting poems and essays in the Spanish language.

José Martí was a man of both thought and action, of love and anger, of poetry and war. This is his story.

BEAUTY AND HORROR · Pepe's parents, Don Mariano Martí and Doña Leonor Pérez, were born in Spain. (*Don* and *Doña* are titles of respect given to men and women in Spanish.) Don Mariano was a sergeant in the Spanish Army and was transferred to Cuba in 1850. Two years later he married Doña Leonor. Pepe, their first of six children, was born on January 28, 1853, in Cuba's capital city of Havana. Pepe's full name was José Julián Martí Pérez, following the Spanish and Latin American custom of using first the father's and then the mother's last name.

The Martí family was poor. Pepe's father often changed jobs, partly due to bad luck, partly due to a

*Pepe's parents, Don Mariano Martí
and Doña Leonor Pérez.*

quick temper. As soon as Pepe's five younger sisters
were old enough, they had to help out by sewing to
bring in money for the household.

Pepe helped as well. When Pepe was nine, Don
Mariano found police work in Hanabana, a stretch of
sugarcane country in Matanzas, east of Havana. The job

required much paperwork. It was summer, so Pepe was off from school. Since Pepe had excellent penmanship, he gave his father a hand.

During the summer Pepe grew to love the countryside. He also worked taking care of a horse he rode and fed every day. When Pepe rode the horse, he saw Cuba's lush, green landscape. Tall sugarcane swayed in the breeze; the tops of huge palm trees seemed to burst in the sunlight.

The towering palms and sugarcane fields of Cuba's countryside found their way into many of the poems and essays Martí later wrote.

But not everything Pepe saw was beautiful. One day, while riding his horse, he saw a tree with thick branches. On it grew some little flowers that looked like small bright-orange flames. Something hung from the tree. As he drew closer, Pepe realized it was the body of a man! He had been a slave who had tried to escape from his owner. The owner sent out men to recapture him. When Pepe saw how the slaves who wanted their freedom were treated, he vowed that through "my life and my actions I will wash away this crime."

AN OPENING AND CLOSING WORLD · At the age of twelve, José Martí became a student of Rafael María Mendive. Mendive was a poet, translator, journalist, and teacher. He excelled in the art of developing children's minds. Mendive was

One thing Pepe hated about Cuban life was slavery. Here black slaves cut sugarcane. If slaves didn't work hard enough or resisted, they were whipped, beaten, and sometimes killed.

also a man with great love for his people. He believed in Cuban independence from Spain. Pepe became Mendive's helper. He was also allowed to borrow books from Mendive's extensive library. The books he read opened the world for him. Years later he would say: "Books console, calm, prepare, enrich, and redeem us."

In the afternoons he would attend discussions of educated young men who were also students of Mendive. Their talks ranged in subject from the work of Spanish poets, to newspaper articles on farming, to the heated world of politics.

Inspired by his teacher's example, Pepe began by taking poems in English by Lord Byron and William Shakespeare and translating, or putting them, into Spanish. Mendive was pleased at how smart, hardworking, and talented Pepe was. When it was time for Pepe to go to high school, the teacher offered to pay his way, since the family was poor and had no way to pay for his education.

Soon Pepe began writing his own poetry. His first poem was published on April 14, 1868, in the newspaper *El Album.* It was addressed to Micaela Mendive, his teacher's wife. The couple had just lost their one-year-old son, Miguel Angel. The poem is a sad and tender remembrance. Ten years after this modest beginning, Martí's poetry would be considered among the most creative in the Spanish language.

A great influence in young Martí's life was this man (above), Rafael María Mendive.

The medal Pepe wears in this photo (right) was the first prize he ever received for his poetry.

That same year, on October 10, in the far-eastern town of Yara, Carlos Manuel de Céspedes began Cuba's war for independence. De Céspedes had been a land-owner who had slaves. He freed them and called for a free Cuba with free people. He asked all Cubans to join in the struggle. The news was received with great excite-ment by Pepe and his friends in Havana.

In Latin America only the Spanish colonies of Cuba and Puerto Rico and the country of Brazil still practiced slavery. The recent Civil War in the United States (1861–1865) had successfully ended slavery there. This made the slaveholders of Cuba nervous. The Spanish captain general of Cuba, Francisco de Lersundi, vowed that the island would remain part of Spain and that slavery would continue. He called for reinforcements.

In January of 1869 the war was still raging. It was about to slam the door on Pepe's opening world. Mendive and Pepe were attending a play at the Villanueva Theater. As the curtain fell and the audience clapped, cries from the public could be heard: "Long live freedom!" and "Long live Carlos Manuel de Céspedes!" Members of the Volunteers shouted back, "Long live Spain!" (Volunteers were a Spanish police force.)

Fighting broke out, and then shots were fired. As people fled the theater, other Volunteers rounded up and attacked people in the streets. They set fires to homes. Several people died. Mendive and Pepe were barely able to escape. They went to Mendive's house. Later that night there was a knock on the teacher's door. They wondered who it was: the police? Volunteers who wanted to drag them away? It was Pepe's mother, Doña Leonor! Relieved, Pepe collapsed in her arms.

A few days later Mendive was arrested in connection with the Yara revolt and the incidents at the Vil-

*Cubans flee as violence breaks out in front of
the Villanueva Theater in this sketch. The incident
changed the course of young Martí's life.*

lanueva Theater. After several months in prison he was
deported to Spain. Martí was without a teacher, spiritual
master, and artistic guide. He felt lost. Fortunately, he
had his best friend, Fermín Valdés, a medical student
whom he had known since he was nine. Fermín would
remain a lifelong friend, and later Martí said that ''love
has not, to my recollection, given me any supreme moment; friendship has.''

Some months later, Pepe was at Fermín's house when Volunteers were passing nearby. The Volunteers heard laughter coming from the house and grew angry at the thought that they were being laughed at. They searched the house and found a letter written by Pepe and Fermín. The letter criticized a fellow student who had joined the Spanish Army. Martí was jailed on October 21, 1869.

At his trial Martí protected his friend Fermín by taking full blame for the letter. On March 4, 1870, he was sentenced by the military court to six years of hard labor breaking rocks. From jail he sent his mother a photograph of himself with chains around his waist and ankle. On the back of it he wrote: "Look at me, Mother, and through your love, don't cry. If it's because I'm a slave to my youth and ideas that I've filled your suffering heart with thorns, remember that among the thorns grow the flowers."

EUROPE AND THE AMERICAS · On January 15, 1871, Martí was deported to Spain, where he was set free. Deeply moved by his prison experience, Martí wrote an article condemning what had happened to him. He began by saying: "Endless pain should be the only name given to these pages. Endless pain, because the pain of being in prison is the rudest, most terrible of pains, the type that kills off intelligence, dries up the soul, and leaves in it scars that can never be erased."

Yet José Martí went on to write that the bitterness of that experience did not teach him to hate. Instead, he pleaded with the Spanish people to free Cuba. He trusted that they would not allow injustices in their name. The rest of Martí's life would be dedicated to healing the scars of prison and to making Cuba a free country.

Martí took advantage of his time in Spain to study law, philosophy, and literature. In his first year of studies he learned that the Volunteers had killed eight medical students in Havana. He thought that Fermín could be one of them! Luckily, he was not, but he was arrested and deported to Spain, where he joined Martí.

During his student years, Martí wrote many articles on Cuban independence and tried to win the Spanish government's support for his cause. He also became known as a skilled speaker.

As he was finishing his studies, Martí learned that his family was moving to Mexico. He left Spain to join them. But bad news awaited him. His favorite sister, Anita, had died. His first poem to be published in Mexico was in her memory. He found love in Mexico as well: In December 1875 he met Carmen Zayas Bazán, who was also Cuban. The couple planned to marry.

Carmen Zayas Bazán,
whom Martí married
on December 20, 1877.

Before getting married, however, Martí had to flee Mexico. A strict ruler, Porfirio Díaz, had seized power and become president. Martí criticized this in a Mexican newspaper and feared punishment. He went south, to Guatemala, but without Carmen. Later he returned to Mexico to marry her and take her back to Guatemala. There, Martí learned the Zanjón Treaty had brought an end to de Céspedes's war of independence. Ten years of struggle had been costly: 200,000 dead and millions of pesos spent. Still Cuba was not free.

Martí and Carmen, who was then pregnant, returned to Cuba. Their son, José Francisco, was born there. Then in August 1879, Cuban rebels again began fighting. Their efforts were brave, but the Cuban people were just not strong enough to face the Spanish so soon after the previous war.

Martí continued to push for the cause of independence. His speeches were becoming well known and commented on by many. Seeing him as a troublemaker, Spanish authorities threw him out of the country again. The rebel uprising faded in a few months. Martí would not return to Cuba for many years.

CUBAN PROBLEMS, AMERICAN LESSONS · During the time Martí spent away from his homeland, he traveled in both North and South America. Living in such different places as New York City and Caracas, Venezuela, he learned much about the many peoples that made up the Americas and their ways. Maybe these lessons, he thought, could help him win Cuba's liberty.

Why had Cuba failed to become free? he wondered. Besides money and training, the Cuban people lacked unity. Cuba was and still is a place of many races. Many black ex-slaves fought in de Céspedes's war. Some whites thought that if the war were won, blacks would try to rule whites. Such thinking divided people fighting for independence.

While Martí was living in Guatemala, he had seen how people of different races contributed to the country. People descended from the Maya—Native Americans of Central America—brought to the country's way of life a sense of the importance of community. They enriched the country for everyone who lived there, including those of Spanish background. This impressed Martí. He later wrote:

A human being has no special rights by belonging to one race or another: It's enough to say human *and it means all rights. All that divides men, all that singles them out, sets them apart and cages them in, is a sin against humanity. . . . A human being is more than being white, being mulatto [a mixture of white and black], being black. Being Cuban means being [more than all of these].*

Something else divided Cubans: unequal wealth. There were a few very rich people and a lot of very poor people. The rich looked down on the poor. The poor felt cheated by the rich. Martí believed that for Cuba to be just and equal, there must be cooperation between the rich and the poor. Martí did not think that this meant taking money from the rich, although he said: "It is better to have good for many than the opulence [too much wealth] of a few." Instead he called for educating the poor and providing them with opportunity. "Until the workers are learned men, they will not be happy," he said.

During the years he spent in the United States, Martí admired the opportunity that seemed to be open to all. "There has never been a happier [people] . . . nor any that created and enjoyed greater wealth," he wrote.

Yet he wondered if the United States' heated "rivalry for wealth" would end up dividing its people.

Martí believed that countries like Guatemala and the United States had much to teach Cuba. Yet he knew that Cuba would have to find its own way of uniting its people based on its own past. Otherwise, the island would be like a tree without roots: It would not grow.

GROWING · During the time he lived in New York City—from 1881 to 1895—Martí grew as a writer and as a fighter for Cuban freedom. He wrote for such New York magazines and newspapers as *The Hour* and *The New York Sun*. He also contributed to over twenty Latin-American newspapers, such as Mexico's *El Partido Liberal*, and Uruguay's *La Opinión Pública*.

Martí wrote on any subject: drugstores, presidential elections, a Chinese funeral, crime. His words were like sparks and set readers' minds ablaze with pictures and ideas. Through his work, Latin Americans learned about the United States as they never had before. He became the most widely read writer in the Americas.

During his New York years Martí published his first book of poems, *Ismaelillo*. It was dedicated to his four-year-old son. These poems—and those published in a later book, *Versos Libres (Free Verses)*—began a whole new style of writing in Spanish. This style was given the name *modernismo*, or modernism.

Martí with his son José.

Martí also worked on a magazine for children. In it, Martí wrote about "Nuestra América," or "Our America." Martí used the expression Nuestra América to refer to Latin America. He described Nuestra América as a place where people speak Spanish, Portuguese, and many native languages like Maya, Quiché, Quechua, Aymará, and Guaraní; and where there is a mix of Native-American, European, and African blood. To Martí, although Canada and the United States were also America, they were different in their ways from Nuestra América.

Martí talked about Nuestra América's heroes so that children would have pride in their Latino heritage. He wrote about Simón Bolívar, José de San Martín, and Miguel Hidalgo. He also spoke of the wonderful Maya, Aztec, and Inca civilizations that existed for thousands of years before the Spanish arrived. Martí collected these stories in a book called *La Edad de Oro* ("The Golden Age"). For many years it was the most famous children's book in all of Latin America.

The front cover of an issue of the children's magazine Martí wrote. It was called La Edad de Oro, *like the book that was a collection of articles from it.*

"NEW PINES" · Unfortunately, there was less and less time to write. Spreading word of the need to free Cuba took up almost all of Martí's time. He traveled to many parts of the United States to rally Cubans living in Philadelphia, Atlanta, New Orleans, and San Antonio. He visited Tampa several times. In this Florida city many Cubans worked in the tobacco industry. On November 26, 1891, Martí gave a moving speech in which he spoke of the need to prepare for war against Spain. It was not to be a war of hate, he said. It was to be an act of love

LA GUANTANAMERA

In 1891, Martí wrote a book of poems called *Versos Sencillos (Simple Verses)*. It tells of his admiration of nature, his love of Cuba, the importance of friendship, and his feelings about injustice. He also wrote about poverty, racism, and how art teaches us important things about life. This is one of the poems in the book.

I am sincere and open
From where palms grow.
Before I'm gone, listen,
From my heart the verses flow.

Yo soy un hombre sincero
De donde crece la palma,
Y antes de morirme quiero
Echar mis versos del alma.

They say a jeweler must
Choose the best gem with pride.
I'll choose a friend I trust
And let love be put aside.

Si dicen que del joyero
Tome la joya mejor,
Tomo a un amigo sincero
Y pongo a un lado el amor.

With the poor of the earth
I wish that my lot may be:
The mountain brook to me is worth
More than the mighty sea.

Con los pobres de la tierra
Quiero yo mi suerte echar:
El arroyo de la sierra
Me complace más que el mar.

I sleep on my bed of stone
My sweet and deep dream:
A bee near my mouth drones,
In my body the world beams.

Duermo en mi cama de roca
Mi sueño dulce y profundo:
Roza una abeja mi boca
Y crece en mi cuerpo el mundo.

Many years after Martí's death, a Cuban composer put music to the words and the song became known as "La Guantanamera." It is the most popular song in Cuba and is known throughout the world. The American folksinger Pete Seeger also arranged it and made it into a popular tune in the 1960s.

Cuban folk bands, like this one, still play "Guantanamera"
and other Martí poems set to music.

Standing in front of the Cuban flag, Martí gives a speech about Cuban freedom. He gave many such speeches throughout the United States, persuading Cubans and others to support his cause.

for Cubans, not only for their country but for their future. Martí even invited Spaniards to help the Cubans, for he knew there were many who wanted Cuba to be free. Knowing that every Cuban needed to be part of this effort, he finished by saying: "With all, and for the good of all."

The next night was the twentieth anniversary of the killing of the medical students, which his friend Fermín Valdés had barely survived. Martí gave another speech and spoke about sacrifice. To him those students had sacrificed their lives and made Cuba's soil rich for future generations who wanted freedom. Because of their deaths, the new generations could flourish, like pine trees. He finished his speech with these words: "Suddenly the sun burst through a clearing in the woods, and there, in that shimmering of sudden light, I saw, standing tall over the yellowish grass, lush branches of the new pines. That's what we are: new pines!"

With these two speeches, Martí won over the Cuban community in Tampa. The speeches were printed and quickly handed out. Cubans everywhere began to respond to the call for independence. Finally, the long years of patient work were starting to pay off.

In January 1892, Martí helped create the Cuban Revolutionary Party. This organization united all Cubans, regardless of race, creed, or class, in a battle for freedom from Spain. Martí was named its president.

Martí spent the next three years planning an uprising to throw Spain out of Cuba. He needed money, so he continued to visit many cities, speaking to Cubans. He needed the support of generals from the earlier uprisings, so he visited Antonio Maceo in Costa Rica and Máximo Gómez in the Dominican Republic. He needed to find out about conditions inside Cuba, so he sent spies to gather information on Spain's military.

The uprising was set for January 1895. Three ships with arms and ammunition were supposed to land in Cuba. Martí would join Gómez in the Dominican Republic. The two would then go to Cuba. Fighting was to begin in three different regions of the island, under the leaderships of Antonio Maceo, Serafín Sánchez, and Máximo Gómez.

Then a traitor informed the U.S. government of the plan. For many years members of the U.S. government thought the country should help Cuba become independent from Spain. That way the United States could have its say in what went on in Cuba. Others, including President William McKinley, believed fighting in Cuba threatened the United States.

On their way to Cuba, the ships were stopped by authorities in Florida. Luckily, Martí was able to collect most of his men's weapons. New plans were made, and by the end of January, Martí was off to join forces with Máximo Gómez.

THE SPANISH-AMERICAN WAR

By the time José Martí and his followers started their uprising in 1895, the United States was Cuba's largest trading partner. It had $50 million invested in the island's land, companies, and businesses. Because of these interests there was much support in the United States for the Cuban patriots. The U.S. battleship *Maine* was sent to protect American lives and property in Cuba during the uprising. On February 15, 1898, the *Maine* blew up in Havana harbor. The United States suspected Spain of causing the explosion. After months of bitter words, Spain declared war on the United States on April 24. A week later American troops invaded Cuba. Although the war is called the Spanish-American

The Maine *exploding in Havana harbor.*

War, thousands of Cubans fought courageously and died in it for their own independence. In four months the Spanish army was defeated.

On December 10, 1898, Spain and the United States signed the Treaty of Paris. As a result, Cuba became independent from Spain. The United States received from Spain the territories of Guam, Puerto Rico, and the Philippines.

As they traveled to Cuba, the two men narrowly avoided disaster. They had to pay money to customs officials, change ships, and finally go on a German fruit ship to avoid being caught by Spanish ships. Finally Martí and Gómez arrived in Cuba in a rowboat, after spending many hours in a storm. Martí was finally back in his native land! When he saw the sugarcane stalks and the palm trees, he wrote in his diary:

In the sugar fields I felt with a son's love the wonder of the [peace] of the glowing night and the palms grouped as if resting one against the other, and the stars shining on their crests. It was like a perfect and sudden cleanness, and the revelation of the universal nature of man.

In a few days Martí joined the newly organized rebel forces. He was named "General of the Liberating Army." It was May 1895. Spanish troops were nearby, and the Cubans began fighting fiercely to drive them back. Martí went with his troops to join in the battle.

The Spaniards, however, prepared a trap. On May 19, Martí and an aide were galloping toward the battlefield at Dos Ríos through smoke and tall trees. They were surprised by shots. Bullets ripped through Martí, and he fell off his horse. The aide, Angel de la Guardia, tried to carry the bleeding Martí but couldn't. Martí died and his body was captured by the Spanish. Cuba had lost its greatest patriot. He was buried a week later, on May 27, in Santiago.

Cuba's man of poetry and soldier of freedom is struck down as he rides into battle at Dos Ríos.

Despite Martí's death, Cubans fought on with great courage for three more years and won their independence. Martí's example became an inspiration for many generations of Cubans. He is still honored in Cuba and in all of Latin America for his courage, his sincerity, his great love of people, his spirit of sacrifice, and his extraordinary poetry and writings. Like a pine tree, he stands tall against injustice and pain, and even taller for life and dignity.

IMPORTANT DATES

1853	Born on January 28 in Havana, Cuba.
1868	On April 14, publishes first poem in the newspaper *El Album.* On October 10, Carlos Manuel de Céspedes begins the war for independence.
1869–1871	Jailed and sentenced to hard labor, then deported to Spain.
1875–1878	Lives in Mexico and meets Carmen Zayas Bazán. Flees Mexico for Guatemala. Marries Carmen. They go to Cuba, where their son is born.
1881–1890	Writes for many magazines and newspapers in New York City. Publishes *Ismaelillo* and *Versos Libres.*
1891–1892	On November 27, 1891, gives speech on the twentieth anniversary of the killing of the Havana medical students. Creates the Cuban Revolutionary Party and plots an uprising against Spain.
1895	On April 11, returns to Cuba to lead the uprising. On May 19, killed in battle at Dos Ríos.

FIND OUT MORE ABOUT JOSÉ MARTÍ

José Martí. Milwaukee: Raintree, 1988.

José Martí by Ted Appel. New York: Chelsea House, 1992.

ABOUT CUBA

Cuba by Ronald Cummins. Milwaukee: Gareth Stevens, 1991.

Cuba by Gail B. Stewart. New York: Macmillan, 1991.

ABOUT THE SPANISH-AMERICAN WAR

The Spanish-American War by Albert Marrin. New York: Macmillan, 1991.

The Story of the Sinking of the Battleship Maine by Zachary Kent. Chicago: Childrens Press, 1988.

INDEX

Page numbers in *italics* refer to illustrations.